Water
as a Gas

by Helen Frost

Consulting Editor: Gail Saunders-Smith, Ph.D.

Reviewer: Carolyn M. Tucker
Water Education Specialist
California Department of Water Resources

Pebble Books

an imprint of Capstone Press
Mankato, Minnesota

Pebble Books are published by Capstone Press
818 North Willow Street, Mankato, Minnesota 56001
http://www.capstone-press.com

Library of Congress Cataloging-in-Publication Data
Frost, Helen, 1949–
    Water as a gas/by Helen Frost.
    p. cm.—(Water)
    Includes bibliographical references and index.
    Summary: Simple text presents facts about the properties and behavior of water
in the state of a gas.
    ISBN 0-7368-0412-9
    1. Water vapor, Atmosperic—Juvenile literature. [1. Steam. 2. Water vapor,
Atmospheric. 3. Water.] I. Title. II. Series: Frost, Helen, 1949– Water.
QC915.F76   2000
530.4′24—dc21   99-14311
                                                                            CIP

Note to Parents and Teachers

The Water series supports national science standards for understanding the properties of water. This book describes and illustrates water as a gas. The photographs support early readers in understanding the text. This book introduces early readers to subject-specific vocabulary words, which are defined in the Words to Know section. Early readers may need assistance to read some words and to use the Table of Contents, Words to Know, Read More, Internet Sites, and Index/Word List sections of the book.

Table of Contents

solid   liquid   gas

4

Water can be a solid,
a liquid, or a gas.
Water as a gas is called
water vapor. You cannot
see water vapor.

6

Heat changes water from a liquid into a vapor. The sun heats water. Water vapor rises into the air. This action is evaporation.

Evaporation makes
wet things dry. Wet
clothes dry in the sun.

More heat makes water
evaporate fast. Puddles
dry up fast on hot days.

Water vapor turns into a liquid when it cools. This action is condensation.

Condensation can form clouds. Clouds are dust and tiny drops of water.

Humid air holds a lot
of water vapor. Humid
air feels wet.

Boiling water makes steam. Steam is water vapor mixed with tiny drops of water.

People use steam
to iron clothes.

Words to Know

boil—to heat water or another liquid until it bubbles; water boils when it reaches 212 degrees Fahrenheit (100 degrees Celsius); water gives off steam when it boils.

condense—to change from a gas into a liquid

evaporate—to change from a liquid into a gas

gas—a substance, such as air, that spreads to fill any space that holds it; water as a gas is called water vapor.

humid—damp and moist; humid air holds a lot of water vapor.

liquid—a substance that flows freely; water as a liquid fills oceans, lakes, and rivers.

solid—something that holds its shape; ice and snow are examples of water as a solid.

Read More

Berger, Melvin and Gilda Berger. *Water, Water Everywhere: A Book about the Water Cycle.* Discovery Readers. Philadelphia: Chelsea House Publishers, 1999.

Farndon, John. *Weather.* Eyewitness Explorers. New York: DK Publishing, 1998.

Fowler, Allan. *What Do You See in a Cloud?* Rookie Read-about Science. New York: Children's Press, 1996.

Jacobs, Marian B. *Why Does It Rain?* Library of Why? New York: PowerKids Press, 1999.

Internet Sites

Heat and Evaporation
http://www.fi.edu/qanda/amy1/amy1.html

Kids' Stuff
http://www.epa.gov/ogwdw/kids/index.html

The Water Cycle at Work
http://www.epa.gov/ogwdw/kids/cycle.html

Index/Word List

Word Count: 127
Early-Intervention Level: 15

Editorial Credits

Mari C. Schuh, editor; Timothy Halldin, cover designer; Kimberly Danger,
   photo researcher

Photo Credits

David F. Clobes, cover, 20
Diane Meyer, 18
Jack Glisson, 4
James P. Rowan, 1
Kate Boykin, 12
Photri-Microstock, 6, 14
Richard B. Levine, 16
Unicorn Stock Photos/Jean Higgins, 8
Visuals Unlimited, 10

Acknowledgments

Special thanks to Dr. Josué Njock Libii of Purdue University-Fort Wayne in
Fort Wayne, Indiana, for his helpful assistance with this book.